rockschool®

Ukulele

US Level 8 (UK Grade 8)

Performance pieces, technical exercises, supporting tests and in-depth guidance for Rockschool assessments

All accompanying and supporting audio can be downloaded from: *www.rslawards.com/downloads*

Input the following code when prompted: **KR5BJHKE2Q**

For more information, turn to page 5

www.rslawards.com

Acknowledgements

Published by RSL Awards Ltd. © 2020
Catalogue Number: RSK200133US
ISBN: 978-1-78936-182-7
Initial US Release | Errata details can be found at *www.rslawards.com/errata*

SYLLABUS
Syllabus designed and written by Jono Harrison
Syllabus Director: Tim Bennett-Hart
Syllabus Consultants: Ashley Hards and Samantha Muir
Hit Tune arrangements by Ashley Hards, Giorgio Serci, Jono Harrison, Calum Harrison & Nat Martin
Supporting Tests written by Jono Harrison and Ashley Hards

PUBLISHING
Proof reading of arrangements by Jono Harrison, Ashley Hards & Calum Harrison
Music engraving, book layout and cover updates by Simon Troup and Jennie Troup of Digital Music Art
Fact files written and edited by Abbie Thomas
Proof reading and copy editing by Jono Harrison, Calum Harrison & Rosie Howard
Cover design by Philip Millard of Rather Nice Design
Cover photograph: © Olga Yatsenko (Shutterstock)

AUDIO
Produced by Jono Harrison
Mixed by Ian Caple & Jono Harrison
Engineered by Jono Harrison, Rory Harvey, Pete Riley, Giorgio Serci and Nat Martin
Supporting Tests recorded by Jono Harrison & Andy Robertson

MUSICIANS
Ukulele: Giorgio Serci, Samantha Muir, Nat Martin, Jono Harrison, Rory Harvey & Calum Harrison
Piano and Keyboards: Jono Harrison & Rory Harvey
Drums & Percussion: Pete Riley
Bass & Synth Bass: Rory Harvey
Guitars: Rory Harvey & Jono Harrison
Lead and Backing Vocals: Nick Shirm, Glen Harvey & Katy Virgoe
Additional Programming: Rory Harvey & Jono Harrison

EXECUTIVE PRODUCERS
John Simpson and Norton York

DISTRIBUTION
Exclusive distributors: Hal Leonard

CONTACTING ROCKSCHOOL
www.rslawards.com
Telephone: +44 (0)345 460 4747
Email: *info@rslawards.com*

RSL Awarding the Contemporary Arts

Table of Contents

Introductions & Information

1 Title Page
2 Acknowledgements
3 Table of Contents
4 Welcome to Rockschool Ukulele Level/Grade 8

Rockschool Level/Grade Pieces

7 'Bohemian Rhapsody' ... Queen
17 'Fire' ... Taimane Gardner
25 'Cinema Paradiso' ... Pat Metheny
31 'Holier Than Thou' ... Metallica
39 'Rather Be' ... Clean Bandit
47 'Spain' ... Chick Corea

Technical Exercises

53 Group A | Scales
56 Group B | Arpeggios
57 Group C | Chords
58 Group D | Stylistic Studies

Supporting Tests

64 Section 1 | Quick Study Piece
68 Section 2 | Ear Tests
70 Section 3 | General Musicianship Questions

About Rockschool Assessments

71 Entering Rockschool Assessments
71 Syllabus Guides
71 Performance and Technical Guidance
72 Marking Schemes

Additional Information

73 Ukulele Notation Explained
74 Copyright Information
75 Rockschool Digital Downloads
76 Rockschool Popular Music Theory

Welcome to Rockschool Ukulele Level/Grade 8

Welcome to Rockschool's contemporary Ukulele syllabus 2020. This syllabus is designed to support ukulele players in their progression from Debut up to Level/Grade 8, through an engaging and rigorous pathway covering all the genres, stylistic elements, techniques and musical skills required for success as a contemporary ukulele player.

All elements required to participate in a Rockschool assessment can be found in the level/grade book. These are as follows:

Hit Tune Arrangements

The 2020 syllabus comprises six hit tune arrangements, meticulously researched and benchmarked to meet level/grade standards. The arrangements are devised so as to equip contemporary ukulele players with industry-relevant skills in any performance environment. These include:

- **All Levels/Grades**
  Four *'Session Style'* arrangements – focussing on developing skills required to perform in an ensemble environment, either in the studio or on stage. These arrangements cover accompaniment and lead playing skills.

- **Debut – Level/Grade 3**
  Two *'Duet'* arrangements – instrumental arrangements without a backing band, focussing on melody and accompaniment skills. The duet arrangements have a second part for teaching/ensemble purposes.

  Please note – candidates will only be assessed on the Assessed Part (see notation)

- **Levels/Grades 4–8**
  Two *'Solo'* arrangements, performed without backing track and arranged to test melodic and self-accompaniment skills.

Each Hit Tune arrangement is preceded by a Fact File, giving surrounding context to the piece and the original performers /recording artists.

Furthermore, you will find performance notes giving additional supportive context to get the most out of the pieces.

Technical Exercises

These are divided into groups at all levels/grades as outlined below:

- **Debut – Level/Grade 5** | Divided into ***three*** groups:
  Group A: Scales
  Group B: Arpeggios
  Group C: Chords

- **Levels/Grades 6–8** | Divided into ***four*** groups:
  Group A: Scales
  Group B: Arpeggios
  Group C: Chords
  Group D: Stylistic Studies

Supporting Tests

There are three sections in this part of the assessment. Please note that the sections contain differing elements depending on the level/grade:

Section 1

Sight Reading *or* **Improvisation & Interpretation** | *Debut – Level/Grade 5 only*
At Debut to Level/Grade 5, candidates can choose between the following:

- **Sight Reading** – a test of the musician's ability to read and perform previously unseen material
- **Improvisation & Interpretation** – a test of the musician's ability to develop previously unseen material in a stylistic way and perform improvised passages of melody. The book contains examples of both types of test. Equivalent 'unseen' examples will be provided for the assessment.

Quick Study Piece | *Levels/Grades 6–8 only*
At Levels/Grades 6–8, candidates must perform a previously unseen Quick Study Piece, combining the skills of the Sight Reading and Improvisation & Interpretation tests from earlier levels/grades.

Section 2

Ear Tests
Candidates must take all tests in this section. Ear tests feature at all levels/grades, but the elements differ as outlined below:

- **Melodic Recall** *and* **Rhythmic Recall** tests | *Debut – Level/Grade 3*
- **Melodic Recall** *and* **Harmonic Recall** tests | *Levels/Grades 4–8*

Section 3

General Musicianship Questions
Candidates must answer General Musicianship Questions (GMQ's) at all levels/grades, on one of their chosen pieces from the repertoire section. The nature of the questions differs depending on the level/grade. Please refer to the relevant section of the level/grade book for details.

Audio

All accompanying audio can be downloaded from RSL directly at *www.rslawards.com/downloads*. This includes backing tracks and full mixes of the level/grade pieces, examples of the technical exercises and supporting tests, and click tracks (where applicable). The audio files are supplied as MP3 format, and can be played using any compatible device.

You will need to input this code when prompted: **KR5BJHKE2Q**

Note: If you have purchased a digital version of this book, you will be sent a link through which you can download the accompanying audio.

'Bohemian Rhapsody' | Queen

Album: *A Night at the Opera* (1975)
Label: EMI Parlophone
Genre: Rock

Written by: Freddie Mercury
Produced by: Roy Thomas Baker, Queen
Chart peak: 1 (US)

Background Info

Queen's record company told the band that because of its length (5:55) and non-traditional structure, 'Bohemian Rhapsody' was unlikely to get airplay. Despite the record company pleading with them, Queen refused to cut any sections and the song went on to become a huge success.

At the time of recording, it was the most expensive single ever made and topped the UK charts for 9 weeks, becoming one of the best selling singles of all time. After lead singer Freddie Mercury's death in 1991, the single reached the top of the charts once more.

Brian May has said that whilst the song was largely crafted in the studio, Freddie had the song fully formed in his mind and intended for it to be a mini-mock-opera.Even the production process was complex. The 180 vocal tracks that were overdubbed for the operatic section pushed the limits of the 24-track tape machine in the studio. Each track had to be layered with others then 'bounced down' into sub-mixes to fit onto each track.

In October 2018 Twentieth Century Fox released a blockbuster telling the story of legendary rock star Freddie Mercury, subsequently named 'Bohemian Rhapsody'. It tells of the star's rise to fame, including the dispute with the band's then record label over whether or not the song should be released as a single. The film pays homage to Mercury's genius, with several scenes depicting the unique techniques used to record the worldwide hit that is 'Bohemian Rhapsody'.

Formed in London in 1970, Queen consisted of Freddie Mercury (lead vocals), Brian May (guitar/vocals), John Deacon (bass) and Roger Taylor (drums/vocals). The band quickly became known for their unique identity and style, often merging classic rock with the likes of disco, opera, pop and many other unlikely genres.

He left behind a legacy that included 14 studio albums which all made it into the top ten on the UK album chart. Queen's total album sales are estimated at 170–200 million, placing them on the list of best selling artists of all time.

Performance Notes

This arrangement is based on Jake Shimabukuro's popular rendition, with adaptations where required for the level/grade. As a general approach to this piece, much is left open to the performer so as to offer full opportunities for stylistic approaches. This is also to encourage preparation by listening to other recordings, notably Jake Shimabukuro's own performance and the original record by Queen.

A guide tempo of 80 bpm is given in section A, but with an indication to play *freely*. You can exploit full rhythmic tension and release between each phrase before settling into a new guide tempo of around 75bpm at section B but with a steady pulse. Dynamics are left completely open to interpretation, as are expressive techniques so use the reference recordings to steer your artistic choices. Some spread chords in section A will work well.

It is crucial to ensure that the melody is clear above any accompanying notes throughout, and you can mimick the studio trickery of the Queen version playing with dynamic tricks (such as 'echoes' through the *"mamma mia"* call and responses in measures 64 and 65). Similarly, contrast in articulations should be fully exploited throughout.

The interchanging of odd, compound and simple time signatures of differing lengths will make more sense if you don't over-analyse them and simply look at the overarching musical ideas (see measure 67, where the *"magnifico"* extends through an over-ringing arpeggio across $\frac{7}{8}$ taking us straight back to $\frac{4}{4}$).

Lastly, for emphasis you might wish to experiment with *rasguaedo* flourishes to embellish chords on occasion. This might be best placed in sections where maximum impact is needed, such as measures 89–93 and 97.

Bohemian Rhapsody

Solo

Queen

Words and Music by Freddie Mercury

[19]
[22]
[24]
C
[26]
[28]
[30]

[32]
D
NH
NH
NH
[34]
[37]
[40]
[42]
[44]

[46]
[48]
NH
[50]
[52]
NH
[54]
E
[56]

[60]
[63]
[66]
Let ring
[68]
[70]
[72]

[74]
[76]
Let ring
[78]
[80]
[83]
♩.=70
[85]

[87]
[89]
[91]
[93]
[95]
=60
rit.
[97]

♩=70 a tempo
NH
NH
[99]
[101]
[103]
[106]
[109]
[112]

'Fire' | Taimane Gardner

Song Title: 'Fire'
Album: *Elemental*
Released: 2018

Genre:Folk / World & Country / Hawaiian
Written by: Taimane Gardner
Produced by: Taimane Tauiliili/Bobby Gardner

Background Info

'Fire' is an intricate instrumental track, featuring on Ukulele virtuoso Taimane Gardner's fifth studio album *Elemental*. The song lasts for approximately four minutes and includes a simple instrumentation, consisting of only ukulele, acoustic guitar and percussion. Known on stage simply by her first name, Taimane performs a beautiful lead ukulele part in this composition and to watch, both live and on the music video, she is mesmerizing in the piece.

Taimane was born in Honolulu, Hawaii but interestingly her decent stems from a mixture of cultures, including Hawaiian, Samoan, German, Irish, French and Swedish. This is evident in her composition style, as her music features influences from folk, jazz, flamenco, classical, Hawaiian, funk and so much more.

She was introduced to the ukulele at the young age of 5 and by just 13 years old she had been discovered by American musician and teacher Don Ho ('Tiny Bubbles'). As a teenager she studied at the hand of virtuoso ukulele player and composer Jake Shimabukuro, known for his fast and complex finger work, and soon became known on the Waikiki circuit as a popular local musician. Taimane went on to release her debut album *Loco Princess* at just 16 years old in 2005 and since then has released a further four studio albums. Her fourth release, *We Are Made of Stars* (2015), saw her receive a nomination for Ukulele Album of the Year at the 2016 Na Hoku Hanohano Awards – a ceremony often described as Hawaii's equivalent to the world famous Grammy Awards.

Over the years Taimane has toured internationally, becoming known for performances of both her own compositions and cover medleys. Her popular renditions of songs such as 'Stairway to Heaven' have seen her reach out to the mass market and in 2014 a column praising the versatile musician featured in Guitar World magazine. Taimane is a great example of the success that can be accomplished with both passion and practise, we can only hope that she will continue to compose, record and tour for many years to come.

Performance Notes

Originally recorded on a ukulele with a 4th string tuned to G below the 3rd string, the Rockschool arrangement of 'Fire' has been adapted for re-entrant tuned instruments and at the slightly lower tempo of 120 bpm (versus the blistering 130 bpm of the original).

The arpeggios in section A (outlining G♯dim^7 and Am) require a mix of *legato* and non-*legato* approaches respectively. For the latter, an economy picking (or 'sweep') technique may suit your playing style, but the ultimate goal is to create a smooth and effortless effect. There is a four measure 'tag', an interesting compositional device which takes us into the *staccato* 3rds in section B. These need to be precise and it will take some preparation to secure your fingering here, but this will enable you to keep a relaxed fretting hand in order to execute these at tempo.

In section D, depending on your picking hand style the 16th-note patterns (alternating between fretted 4th string and open 1st) can be approached fingerstyle or with thumb pick using ***p*** [4th] ***i–m*** [3rd]. If holding a flatpick (between ***p*** and ***I***) then the 3rd string notes will need to be played with ***m*** and ***a***. Section G requires *tremolando* picking until section H, and you are at liberty to experiment with the timing and placement of your *tremolando* picking through this passage.

Be sure to observe the ***rallentando*** leading to the slower tempo at section I, which provides dramatic contrast, before *accelerando* takes you back to the original tempo eight measures before the **D.S.** The notated dynamics are crucial to the structure of the piece but there is also room for stylistic interpretation. For instance, a *crescendo* on the repeat of section D would build anticipation; similarly, dynamic swells through section I would add interest to the projection of the melody.

Fire

Taimane Gardner

♩=120 *Folk / World & Country / Hawaiian*

[13]
[15]
B
mf
[17]
[20]
[23]
C
[25]
To Coda
[27]

[29]
[31]
D
mp let ring
[33]
1.
2.
f
[35]
E
[38]
[41]
[44]

F
p
f
[46]
[48]
G
Continue tremolando picking
[50]
† = Tremolando picking (not strictly timed)
(cont. tremolando picking)
[53]
(cont. tremolando picking)
[56]
H
mf
p
[58]
mf
[60]

[63]
mp
[66]
mf
mp
rall.
I
♩=80
[69]
p
[72]
mf
[75]
[78]
accel.
♩=120
[81]
f

D.𝄋. al Coda
[85]
Coda
[89]
[91]
[93]
[95]
f
[97]
mp
NH
[99]

'Cinema Paradiso' | Pat Metheny

Album: *Beyond the Missouri Sky (Short Stories)*
Released: 1996
Label: Verve
Genre: Soundtrack/Jazz
Written by: Andrea Morricone
Produced by: Charlie Haden/Pat Metheny

Background Info

The film score for the 1988 release of 'Cinema Paradiso' was written by Ennio Morricone and his son Andrea Morricone, with credits for the 'Love Theme' being granted to the latter. Both the music and film were extremely well received; this is evident in the huge number of awards won. To name a few, the film and score took 5 BAFTAS at the 1991 ceremony and won both an Oscar and a Golden Globe in 1989.

In 1996, Jazz duo Pat Metheny and Charlie Haden recorded their version of Morricone's 'Love Theme' and featured it on their album *Beyond the Missouri Sky (Short Stories)*. The pair were highly praised for their album release and it saw them taking 'Best Jazz Instrumental' at the 1998 Grammy Awards. As with all tracks on the album, this take on 'Love Theme' features Haden on double bass and Metheny on acoustic guitar (and all other instrumentation). Together, the duo create what can only be described as awe inspiring Jazz duets.

Metheny was born into a musical family and became fascinated with Jazz music at a young age. He launched his debut career in 1976 with the release of *Bright Size Life* and shortly after went on to form the Pat Metheny Group in 1978. Throughout his career he has featured on countless collaborations and side projects and has been involved in over 40 studio album releases. Metheny is praised for his incorporation of progressive, contemporary, Latin and fussion jazz and is often described as a pioneer in the jazz community. His accolades are hugely impressive and include 20 Grammy Awards (to date he is the only artist to have won Grammys in ten different categories), two Echo Awards and a Lifetime Achievement Award from JazzFM.

Charlie Haden was also born into an incredibly musical family and became interested in jazz at the young age of 14. His career spanned over 50 years before he sadly passed away in 2014. Many critics felt that he lead the way for harmonic double bass playing in jazz and his style of plying has been described as "both radical and mesmerizing". In 2013 he was awarded the Grammy Lifetime Achievement Award and in 2015 a ceremony took place in his honour at the French Cultural Services, paying respect to the musician's great talent and accomplishments.

Performance Notes

It is valuable preparation to reference the original Morricone recording as well as Pat Metheny's beautiful arrangement, in order to inform your own stylistic choices. Make sure your melody is clear above the accompanying notes and that the melodic line sounds continuous and not interrupted by the accompaniment. Careful picking control will be needed to achieve the desired effect.

Dynamics have been omitted from this arrangement to provide the opportunity to appropriately develop the shape of the piece. The original Morricone track starts relatively sparsely with the dark tone of the clarinet playing the melody and a string section providing the accompaniment. The melody passes to other orchestral instruments and you will hear the timbre thicken as more of the orchestra is used in the accompaniment as the song develops. Listen for the arpeggiated use of the piano because this may give you ideas how you wish to develop section B on the repeat. Experiment with picking style and hand position (near the bridge, over the neck) to help you create tonal contrast in the different sections. Wide use of dynamics will help you create a varied tonal pallet to make different sections stand out.

The solo section will require chordal or arpeggiated accompaniment. The harmonic structure of this section guides you towards working within the scale of A harmonic minor and C major, but you could experiment with the altered scale over the V^7 chord.

Cinema Paradiso

Session Style

Pat Metheny

From 'Cinema Paradiso' (1988)

♩ = 70 *Soundtrack/Jazz*

D♯dim7
E7sus4
E7♭9
[23]
B
Am
Dm
G7
Csus4
C
Develop melody with arpeggiated accompaniment on D.S.
[26]
Em7/B
Am
Am/G
F
Am/E
[30]
Dm
Dm/C
Bdim7
E7♯9
Am
[34]
C/G
Fmaj9
D7/F♯
Gsus4
[38]
G
Csus4
C
To Coda
[42]

Solo
C
Am7
Dm7
G7
C
[45]
G/B
Am
Am/G
Fmaj7
NH
[49]
Dm7
Bm7♭5
E7♯5♯9
[53]
Am
Am/G
Fadd2
[56]
D♯dim7
E7
[59]
Am7
Dm7
G7
C
Improvise solo (16 measures)
[62]

G/B
Am
Am/G
Fmaj7
[66]
Dm7
Bm7♭5
E7♯5♯9
Am
[70]
Am/G
Fadd2
D♯dim7
E7
D.𝄋. al Coda
[74]
Coda
C/G
G7sus4
C/G
[78]
G7sus4
C/G
G7sus4
[81]
C/G
Fm/G
C
[84]

'Holier Than Thou' | Metallica

Album: *Metallica*
Label: Elektra
Genre: Thrash Metal / Heavy Metal

Written by: James Hetfield And Lars Ulrich
Produced by: Bob Rock, James Hetfield and Lars Ulrich
Chart peak: 1 (US Billboard 200 Chart)

Background Info

'Holier Than Thou' is featured on Metallica's self-titled fifth studio album, also known as *The Black Album*. The record was a massive worldwide success and became Metallica's best-selling album. The record signals a change in Metallica's sound, including a slower and more melodic approach towards heavy metal. The record sold 16 million copies in the US alone, with worldwide sales estimated at 31 million.

The band had frequent disagreements with producer Bob Rock during the recording process. Rock pushed Hetfield to write more involved and personal lyrics and this led to arguments. It did, however, produce a positive result. Unlike previous recordings the band played live in the studio. Their attention to detail and perfectionist approach tested Rock's patience and the album was mixed three times until the band were satisfied. Production costs reached 1 million US dollars. The tension resulting from the sessions made Rock swear he'd never work with Metallica again. Much of this is documented in the documentaries 'A Year and a Half In The Life Of Metallica' and Classic Albums: *Metallica – Metallica*. Rock, against his own predictions, worked with Metallica again on the production of *Load* in 1996, *ReLoad* in 1997 and *St. Anger* in 2003. During the production of *Metallica* drummer Lars Ulrich, bassist Jason Newsted, and lead guitarist Kirk Hammett divorced their wives.

The promotional tour of *Metallica* saw the band play as part of the Monsters Of Rock festival tour for the fourth time. The tour closed in Moscow, Russia, in September 1991 in what was described as the first free outdoor Western rock concert in the country, with estimates of as many as 1.5 million in attendance it was one of the biggest free concert audiences ever. The band followed Monsters Of Rock with the *Wherever We May Roam Tour* in 1992 during which James Heftfield suffered second and third degree burns after accidentally walking into a 3.5 metre flame shot from the stage pyrotechnics set. After recovery the band continued with the *Nowhere Else to Roam Tour*.

'Holier Than Thou' was performed until 1995. When Robert Trujillo joined the band in 2003 Metallica started to perform a more extensive back catalogue and the song was re-introduced to live performances. *Metallica* was played in its entirety during the 2012 *European Black Album Tour*.

Performance Notes

The fast tempo requires a very precise and economical picking hand approach in order to execute the interchanging palm muting and natural passages. This entails very small movements across the strings, which in turn can make it tricky to achieve a full tone. Experimentation will be needed here to achieve a balance between speed and clear projection of sound, and the chord tones will need to be audible through the palm muted passages so it is important not to apply the palm too far in front of the bridge as to deaden the strings.

One of the main challenges throughout the song is timing, with frequent emphasis on beat 4 in many measures, and notes tied across beat 1. This can be a little disorienting at full tempo so be sure to prepare the entire piece at a slower tempo first. Similarly, a displacement of the riff in section C occurs at measure 55 before reverting at measure 58, so it is best to mark up this section in smaller phrases and study it this way before piecing it together.

The solo contains a variety of articulations which again at this tempo will need careful preparation, notably the grace notes in measures 66 and 69, and the timing through measures 75 and 76. It is important not to rush the preparation of the solo, and good practise will be to break down each measure into smaller rhythmic sections so these can be executed with confidence at full tempo.

Holier Than Thou

Session Style

Metallica

E5
Lit - tle whis - pers cir - cle a - round your head. Why don't you wor - ry a - bout your - self in - stead?
TAB
[18]
PM
[22]
G5 E5
Who are you? Where ya been? Where ya from? Gos - sip burn - ing on
[26]
G5 E5
the tip of your tongue. You lie so much you bel - ieve your - self.
[29]
Judge not lest ye be judged your - self
[32]

B
Ho - li - er than thou,
you are.
Ho - li - er than
thou,
you are.
You
know
not.
Yeah!
Who the hell are You?
PM
G5
[35]
[38]
[41]
[44]
[46]

C
E5
[49]
[52]
F5
E5
F5
E5
[55]
F5
F♯5
G5
[58]
G♯5
E5
[61]
D
G5
A5
B♭5
E5
G5
A5
B♭5
[64]

E5
G5
A5
B♭5
E5
[68]
G5
E5
[71]
G5
[74]
[77]
E5
[79]
[83]

E
E5
[87]
Ho - li - er than
[90]
thou,
you are.
You
[93]
know
not.
[96]
G5
E5
Woah,
not!
[99]

'Rather Be' | Clean Bandit

Album: *New Eyes*
Released: 2014
Label: WMG/Atlantic
Genre: Electronic / Classical Crossover/ Dance-Pop

Written by: Jack Patterson / James Napier / Nicole Marshall / Grace Chatto
Produced by: Grace Chatto/Jack Patterson
Chart Peak: 10 (US Billboard Hot 100)

Background Info

'Rather Be' was a hit for British electronic band Clean Bandit, featuring vocals from multimillion selling artist Jess Glynne. Clean Bandit are known for their unique talent of merging classical with electronica and this song is no exception, built around a prominent synth sound which creates a house feel which compliments a beautiful violin and piano section.

The track was written by Clean Bandit's Jack Patterson (keyboard/piano) and Grace Chatto (cello), alongside Nicole Marshall and Ivor Novello award winning songwriter Jimmy Napes. As well as Clean Bandit, Napes is well known for his work with chart topping artists such as Sam Smith, Alicia Keyes and Disclosure.

'Rather Be' was hugely successful for Clean Bandit and gave them their first UK number 1 single, peaking there in January of 2014 and remaining for four weeks.

'Rather Be' broke several download and sales records at its time of release. In 2015 'Rather Be' became only the seventh single ever to be awarded 3 x Platinum by the British Phonographic Industry, several more have now achieved this status but for a January release and first time UK number 1 this was an incredible accomplishment for Clean Bandit. Since its release sales have continued in the UK and 'Rather Be' now holds a 4 x Platinum certification.

A complex song to sing, Jess Glynne proved herself to be an incredibly skilled vocalist and provided a mesmerizing, uplifting and flawless vocal. Her appearances on Clean Bandit's 'Rather Be' and Route 94's 'My Love' (also 2014) saw her rise to success and she went on to release a chart-topping debut album (*I Cry When I Laugh*) in 2015. Her second studio album, *Always In Between*, also proved successful and peaked at number 1 in the UK album charts in 2018. Thanks to the success of this second album Glynne has now become the first British female solo artist to have seven UK number 1 singles.

Performance Notes

This arrangement primarily consists of a repeated section throughout the score, first shown in measures 9 to 16. Within this there are some technical challenges which will require attention. These can be approached in a variety of ways to suit your technical strengths. Here are some suggestions though,

Firstly, throughout measure 10 beat 1, the second fret can be barred with the index finger, allowing the F♯ to be sounded from a pull off. Secondly, beginning on the last eighth-note of measure 11, there is a cluster of six 16th-notes. The second fret can be barred at the same time as the first 16th-note (G♯) of measure 12. This will allow the third 16th-note (F♯) to be sounded from a pull off.

Both of the above approaches may feel a little strange at first as you're essentially barring a group of notes before you need to play them. This can be slowed down for practice. However, if you know the exact notes that are causing trouble, it could also be useful to isolate them (and their surrounding notes) and loop the section at performance tempo. This approach tends to be more successful with small groups of 2-4 notes where memory isn't an issue, and the sole intention is to improve technique.

There are also two areas for development within this score. Firstly, the *'develop on repeat'* section at measure 17-24 occurs during the repeat when the piano drops out. With the piano dropping out, there's a lot more freedom for the Ukulele part. An idea here could be to identify the shapes that are being picked through for each chord. Then experiment with modifying their rhythms and picking patterns, possibly introducing new notes if it sounds suitable. Secondly, *'improvise melody on repeat'* occurs during measures 25-30. A nice idea here is to focus on filling the space in between the vocal lines. This approach can be seen throughout a lot of genres, in particular blues.

Rather Be

Session Style

Clean Bandit

G♯m F♯ E B/D♯ G♯m F♯
I would wait for - ev - er, ex - ult - ed in the scene.
staked out on a mis - sion to find our in - ner peace.
Develop on repeat (measures 17–24)
[17]
E B/D♯ G♯m F♯ E B/D♯
As long as I am with you, so
Make it ev - er - last - ing,
[20]
Emaj7 C♯m
my heart con - tin - ues to beat.
no - thing's in - com - plete.
[23]
Bridge
Emaj7 D♯m7 G♯m11
With ev - 'ry step we take, Ky - o - to to the Bay. Stroll - ing so cas - u - ally.
Improvise melody on repeat (measures 25–30)
Let ring
[25]

Emaj7
D♯m7
We're dif - f'rent and the same, get you an - oth - er name.
[28]
G♯m11
F♯
Switch up the bat - ter - ies.
pp
f
[31]
Chorus
G♯m
F♯
E
B
F♯/A♯
If you gave me a chance I would take it.
[33]
G♯m
F♯
E
B
F♯/A♯
G♯m
F♯
It's a shot in the dark but I'll make it. Know with all of your heart
[35]

E B C♯m7 Emaj7 D♯/F×
— you can't shame me. When I am with you there's no place I'd ra - ther be.
[38]
Gm7 D♯m7 E D♯7♯5/F× Gm7 D♯m7 E
N, n, no, no, no. No place I'd ra - ther be. N, n, no, no, no.
[41]
D♯7♯5/F× G♯m7 D♯m7 E
No place I'd ra - ther be. N, n, no, no, no.
[44]
F♯
Italic lyrics 2° only
No place I'd ra - ther be. When I am with you there's no place I'd ra - ther be.
[46]

Middle 8

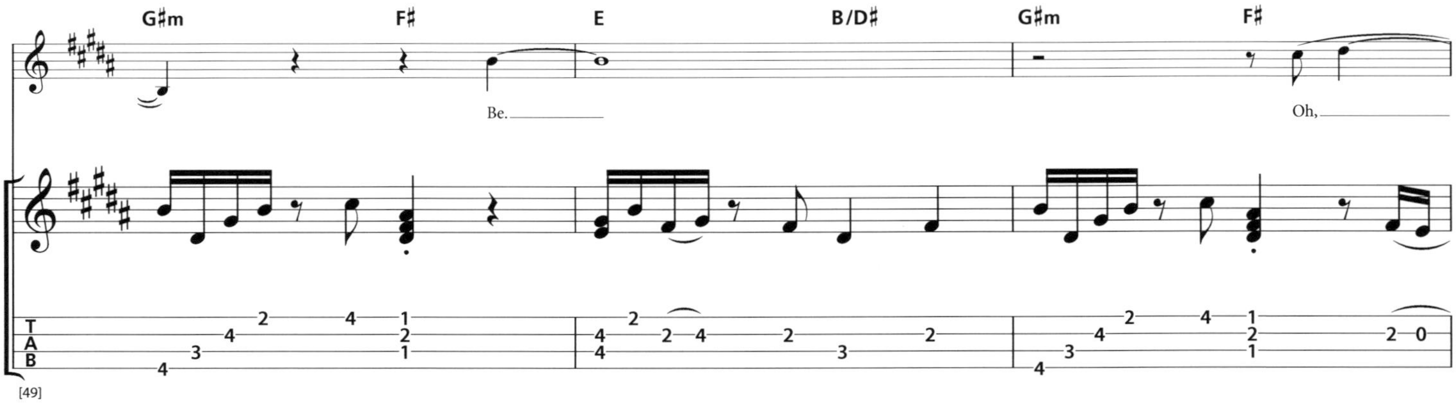

Chorus

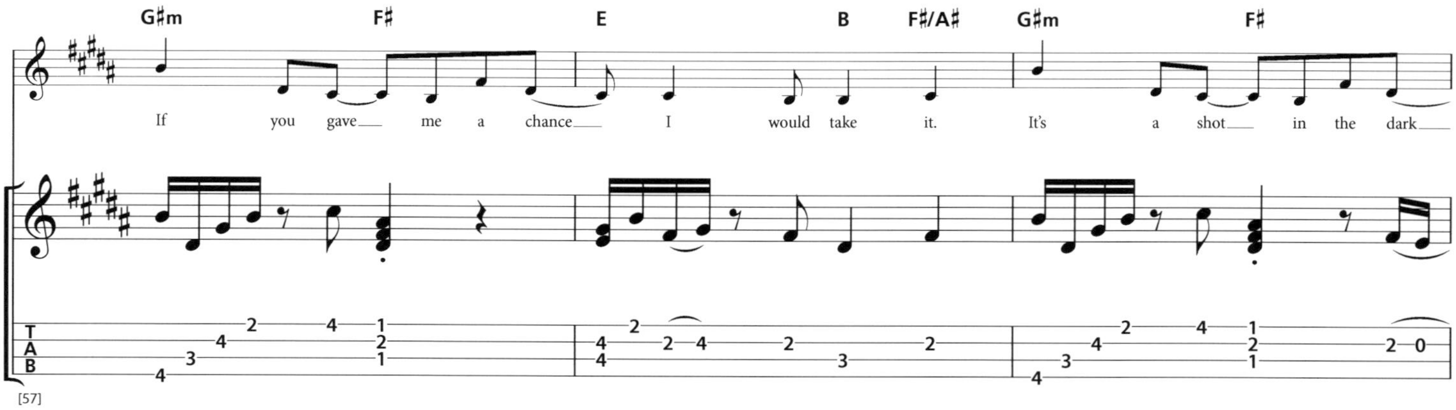

E B F♯/A♯ G♯m F♯ E B
but I'll make it. Know with all of your heart you can't shame me.
[60]
C♯m7 Emaj7 D♯7♯5/F× Gm7 D♯m7
When I am with you there's no place I'd ra - ther be. N, n, no, no, no.
pp f
[63]
E D♯7♯5/B♭ Gm7 D♯m7 E D♯7♯5/F×
No place I'd ra - ther be. N, n, no, no, no. No place I'd ra - ther be.
[66]
G♯m7 D♯m7 E F♯
N, n, no, no, no. No place I'd ra - ther be.
[69]
When I am with you there's no place I'd ra - ther be.
[71]

'Spain' | Chick Corea

Album: *Light as a Feather* (1972)
Label: Polydor
Genre: Jazz Fusion

Written by: Chick Corea
Produced by: Chick Corea
Chart peak: 6 (Billboard Jazz Albums)

Background Info

'Spain' is an instrumental jazz fusion piece written by composer and pianist Chick Corea. 'Spain' is arguably Corea's most recognisable work and is now considered a jazz standard. The original composition featured on the album *Light as a Feather*, the second studio album to be released by Chick Corea and his band Return to Forever.

The *Light as a Feather* recording features performances from Corea (electric piano), Airto Moreira (drums), Flora Purim (percussion), Stanley Clarke (bass) and Joe Farrell (flute). The piece was inspired by Joaquin Rodrigo's 'Concierto de Aranjuez' and actually opens with the adagio taken from the inspirational piece. Corea's composition has been covered and recorded by several other artists and in an array of genres, such as Paco de Lucia's flamenco version and Bela Fleck's bluegrass version in 1979.

Light as a Feather was met with critical acclaim and won several awards, including two Grammys at the 1973 ceremony for Best Instrumental Arrangement (Spain) and Best Jazz Performance by a Group (*Light as a Feather*). These were Corea's first Grammy wins but were certainly not his last, throughout his career he has been nominated for a staggering 65 awards and has won 22.

Chick Corea was born Armando Anthony Corea to Italian and Spanish descent in 1941. His father was a Jazz trumpeter and leader of a Dixieland band in the 1930s and 40s and didn't wait long to pass the torch, introducing his son to the piano at the young age of four. The pianist grew up surrounded by jazz and became heavily influenced by his father and his fellow musicians. By eight years old he had begun learning the drums, which led to his well-known technique of using the piano percussively.

The composer went on to launch his debut career in 1966 with his first studio album *Tones for Joan's Bones*. By the late 60s and early 70s Corea found himself playing with the legendary Miles Davis and became involved in the birth of jazz fusion. His work then moved away from avant-garde to the unique sounds of jazz fusion. Throughout his career Corea has released over 80 studio albums, has participated in countless collaborations and remains a prominent figure in the world of jazz.

Performance Notes

This arrangement captures the essence of Chic Corea's style and displays his instantly recognisable approach to harmony and melody. The piece drew inspiration from Rodrigo's 'Concierto de Aranjuez' and quotes from the melody can be heard throughout the arrangement.

Technical accuracy and dexterity will be of great importance to perform this successfully.

The slow harmonic change in the solo sections provides an excellent chance to explore the chromatic colours that modal playing can produce. The semitone shift from Gmaj to F♯^{7} gives a strong Spanish flavour and the use of G lydian and F♯ phrygian dominant and can really enhance this sound. However, the extended use of these chords will give you the opportunity to explore far more tonal colours within your phrases than using these set modes. It is important your style of phrasing compliments the song and it can help to look at the smooth syncopated melodic lines and rapid leaping phrases seen elsewhere in the song.

Spain

= 140 Jazz Fusion
Intro
Em7add4
F♯♭9
[4]
A
Gmaj7
F♯7
[7]
Em
A7
Dmaj7
Gmaj7
[11]
C♯7
F♯7♯5
Bsus2
Bm
[15]
Unison
[19]

[23]
To Coda
[26]
B
Gmaj7
[30]
F♯7
[34]
Em7
A7
[38]
Dmaj7
Gmaj7
[42]

C♯7
F♯7
3
[46]
Bm7
B7
[50]
C
Solo
Gmaj7
[54]
F♯7
[58]
Em7
A7
[62]
Dmaj7
Gmaj7
[66]

C♯7
F♯7
[70]
Bm7
[73]
B7
1.
2.
[76]
Em
A7
Dmaj7
Gmaj7
[79]
D.C. al Coda
C♯7
F♯7♯5
Bsus2
Bm
[83]
Coda
Gmaj13
F♯7♯5
Bsus4
[87]

Technical Exercises

In this section, you will be asked to play a selection of exercises, chosen by the assessor, from groups A, B, & C.

In Group D you will be asked to prepare one Stylistic Study from the three printed. The choice of stylistic study will determine the style of the Quick Study Piece, for example, if you choose a rock & pop Stylistic Study then the assessor will give you a rock & pop Quick Study Piece in that section of the assessment.

You do not need to memorise the exercises (and can use the book in the assessment) but the assessor will be looking for the speed of your response. The assessor will also give credit for the level of your musicality.

Groups A, B, & C need to be prepared as shown below. Where applicable, the assessor will play the click at the given tempo, and you should begin to play after four clicks.

Group D is played to a backing track.

Group A | Scales
The tempo for this group is ♩=100 bpm.

Exercises 1–3 need to be prepared from the root notes E, F, F♯ and G. The assessor will announce the key for each example.

1. Whole Tone | from the root notes E, F, F♯ or G (E whole tone shown)

2. Diminished | from the root notes E, F, F♯ or G (F diminished shown)

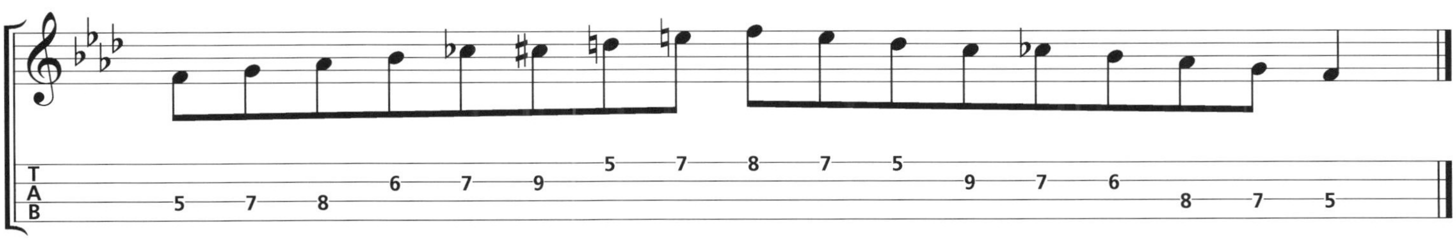

3. Altered | from the root notes E, F, F♯ or G (F altered shown)

Exercises 4–6 need to be prepared in the keys shown only, using the given fingering.

4. Chromatic scale | on one string: starting on G, C, E or A (G shown)

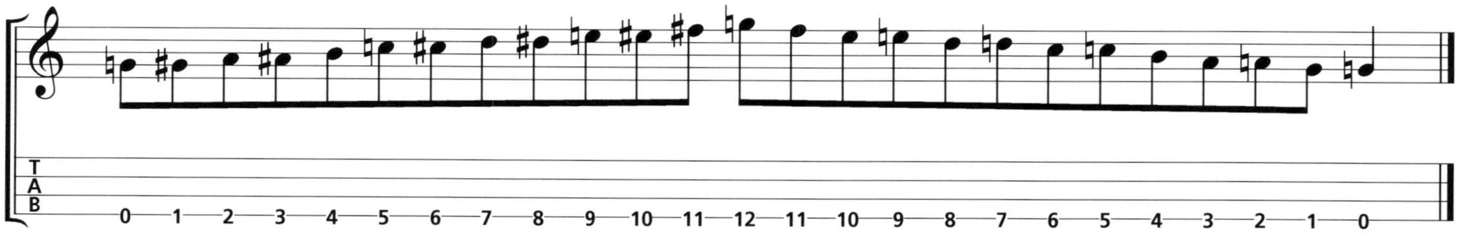

5. E phrygian mode | campanella style

6. C major | in sixths on strings 3 & 4

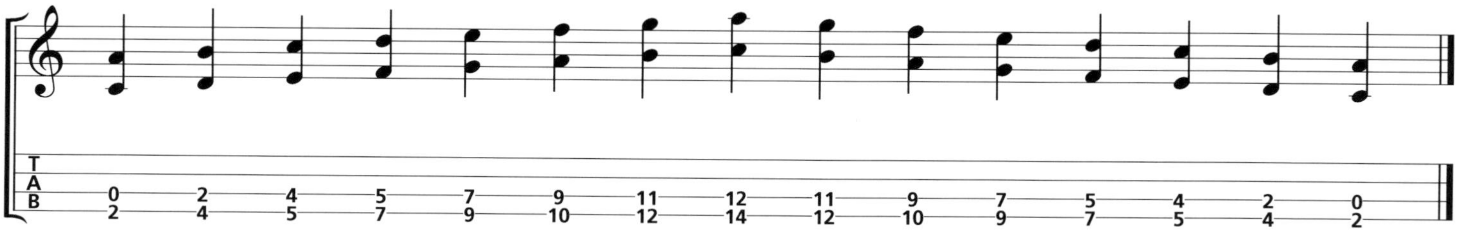

In addition, candidates must prepare the following from previous levels/grades:

1. Linear scales with root notes on any of the four open strings (G, C, E or A):

Major
Natural minor
Melodic minor
Harmonic minor

- Tempo: ♩=100
- One octave
- Eighth notes, finishing on a quarter note.
- Acending and Descending

2. Any of the following scales from previous levels/grades *played campanella style*:

D natural minor
D harmonic minor
E natural minor
E dorian mode
C major
G major

- Tempo: ♩=100
- One octave
- Eighth notes, finishing on a quarter note
- Ascending and descending

Group B | Arpeggios

The tempo for this group is ♩=100 bpm.

Exercises 1–4 need to be prepared from the root notes E, F, F♯ and G. The assessor will announce the key for each example.

1. Dominant 7♯5 arpeggio | from the root notes E, F, F♯ or G (E shown)

2. Dominant 7♭5 arpeggio | from the root notes E, F, F♯ or G (F shown)

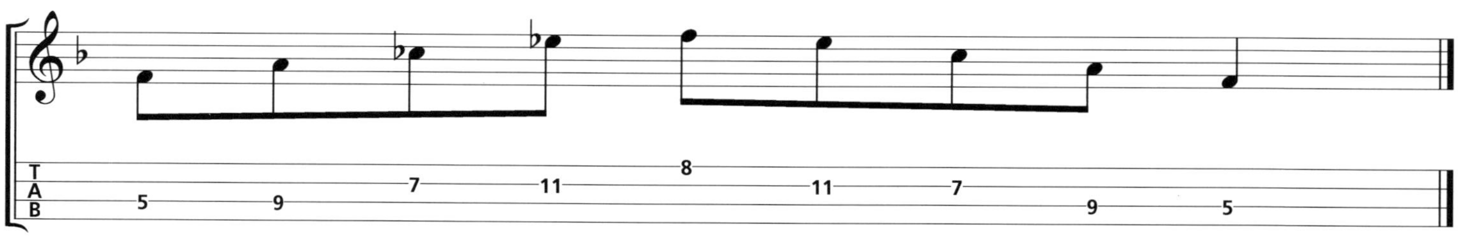

3. Dominant 7♭9 arpeggio | from the root notes E, F, F♯ or G (F♯ shown)

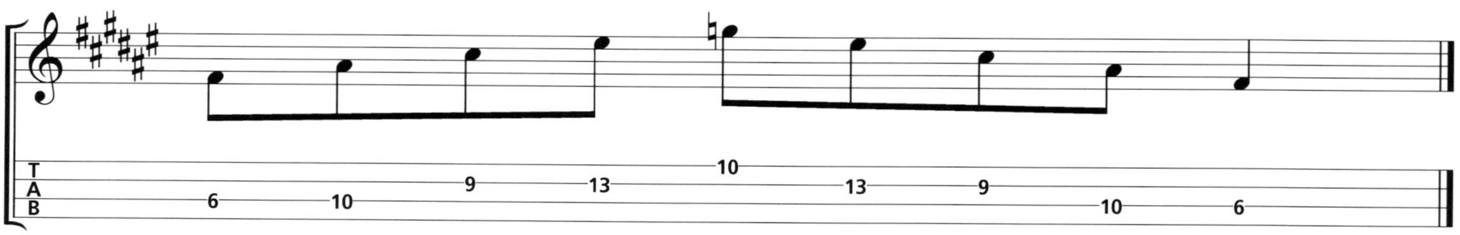

4. Minor/Major 9 arpeggio | from the root notes E, F, F♯ or G (G shown)

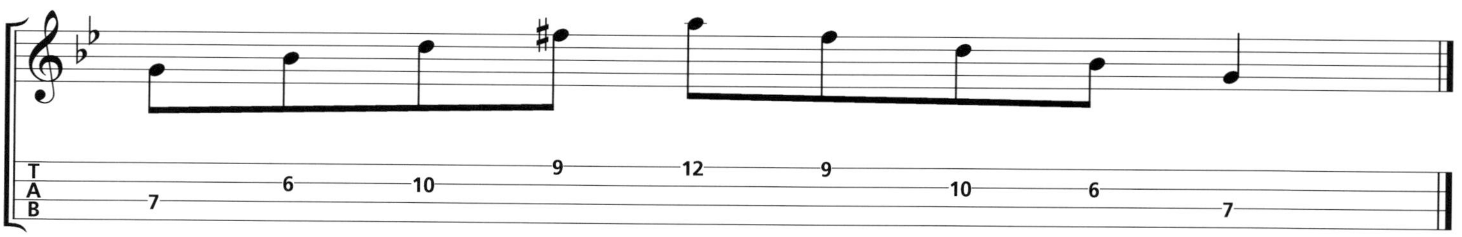

In addition, candidates must prepare the following from previous levels/grades:

E minor 6 arpeggio on four strings
G minor 7 arpeggio on four strings

- Tempo: ♩=100
- One octave
- Eighth notes, finishing on a quarter note
- Ascending and descending

Group C | Chords

The tempo for this group is ♩=100 bpm.

Exercises 1 & 2 need to be prepared in the key of F only. Candidates must perform both voicings to continuous click.

1. Dominant 7♯5 | in the key of F

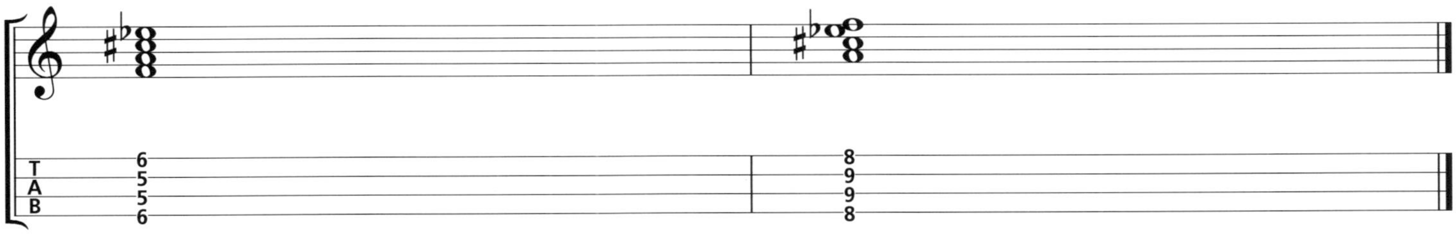

2. Dominant 7♭5 | in the key of F

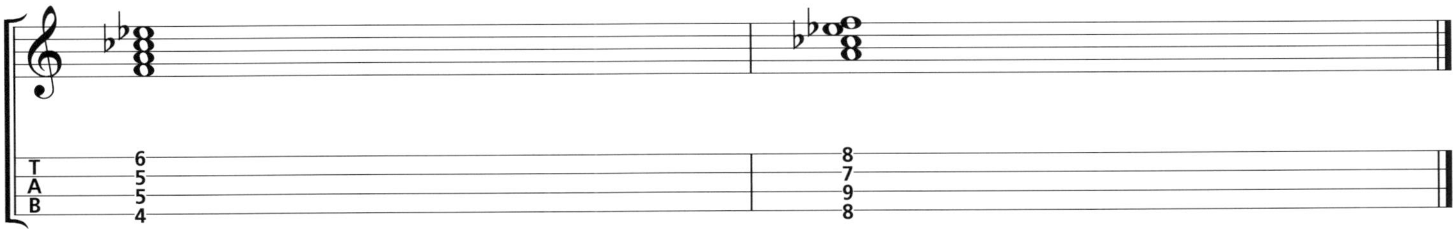

Exercises 3 & 4 need to be prepared in the key of C only and only the voicings shown. Candidates must play the chord when directed by the assessor.

3. Dominant 7♯9 | in the key of C

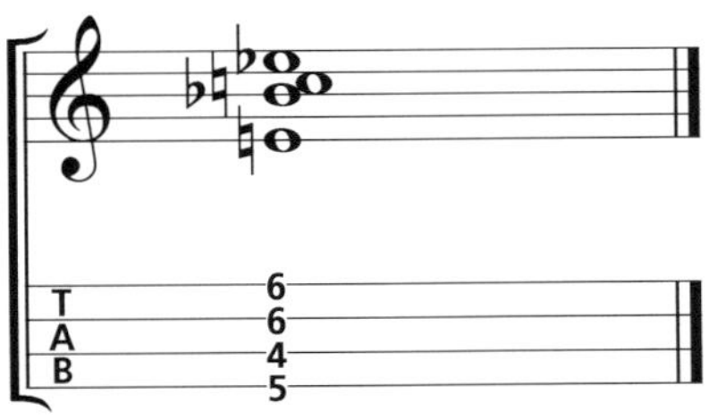

4. Dominant 7♭9 | in the key of C

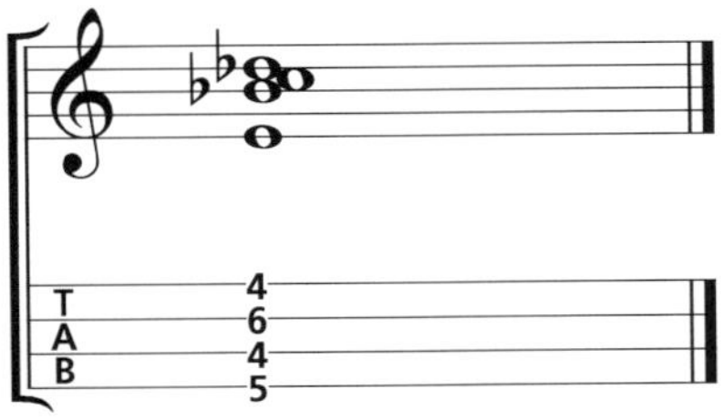

Group D | Stylistic Studies

You will prepare a technical study from one group of styles from the list below and perform it to the backing track. Your choice of style will determine the style of the Quick Study Piece, for example, if you choose a rock & pop Stylistic Study then the assessor will give you a rock & pop Quick Study Piece in that section of the assessment.

Styles:

- Rock and Pop (page 59)
- Soul, Jazz and Blues (page 60)
- Ukulele Specialist (page 62)

♩=114 Neo-Classical Rock
f
Fingerstyle or strum strings (muting those not fretted)
mp (Cresc. on repeat)
ff

♩=100 Fusion
Gm9
T
A
B
G♭9
G♭13
Fm9
B♭13
D♭/E♭
D7♯5♯9

Gm9
G♭9
Fm7
B♭9
D♭/E♭
D7♯5♯9

♩=80 Ukulele Specialist
let ring throughout
p m i p m i p i
f
sp
f sp
f sp
f
p
f
p
f
mp Cresc.
[3]
[5]
[7]

f
mp Cresc.
f
mp Cresc.
[9]
f
mp Cresc.
f
mp Cresc.
[11]
f
pp Cresc. poco a poco
[13]
f
[15]

Supporting Tests

Section 1 | Quick Study Piece

At this level/grade you will be asked to prepare and play a short Quick Study Piece (QSP). Printed below are three examples of the type of QSP you are likely to receive in the assessment. You will be shown the test and played the track with the *notated parts played*. Any measures that require improvisation or development will not be demonstrated. You will then have three minutes to study the test. The backing track will be played twice more. You will be allowed to practise during the first playing of the backing track, with the notated parts now absent, before playing it to the assessor on the second playing of the backing track.

The style of your QSP is determined by the Stylistic Study you selected in the technical exercise section – for example, if you selected a rock and pop Stylistic Study then you will be given a rock & pop Quick Study Piece. The QSP is in the form of a lead sheet and it is up to you to create your own interpretation of the music in the parts where instructed to do so.

The genres for the QSPs are the same those found in the Stylistic Studies:

- Rock and Pop (page 65)
- Soul, Jazz and Blues (page 66)
- Ukulele Specialist (page 67)

♩=90 Funk/Pop
Dm7
G7
2
B♭maj7
A7
Play chordal rhythms
[3]
Dm7
G7
B♭maj7
A7
Dm7
B♭7
Develop
[6]
Dm7
G7
Dm7
Develop solo
[9]
G7
B♭maj7
A7
[12]
Dm7
G7
B♭maj7
A7
Dm7
[15]

♩=130 Jazz
A♭maj7 Fm7 B♭m7 E♭7♭9 Cm7 Fm7
Play written melody
B♭m7 Gdim7 A♭ Fm7 B♭m7 E♭7
Improvise melody
[4]
C7 F7 B♭m7 E♭7 A♭maj7 Fm7
[7]
B♭m7 E♭7 Cm7 F♯dim7 B♭m7 Gdim7
Develop chord vamp
[10]
C7 F7 B♭m7 E♭9 A♭maj7 A♭maj7
[13]

♩=75 Ukulele Specialist
Em
Let ring
Cmaj7
Em
Develop campanella melody using rhythms shown
[3]
C
B7
Play melody
[5]
Am
B7
Improvise melody over chords
[7]
Cmaj7
Bdim7
Play chordal rhythms
[9]
Am
B7
Em
Develop chordal rhythms
[11]

Section 2 | Ear Tests

There are two Ear Tests in this level/grade. The assessor will play each test to you twice. You will find one example of each type of test printed below.

Test 1: Melodic Recall

The assessor will play you a two measure melody with a bass and drum backing using the F major, F harmonic minor or F natural minor scale. The first note of the melody will be *either* the root note *or* fifth and the first interval will be *either* ascending *or* descending. You will play the melody back on your instrument. You will hear the test twice.

Each time the test is played the sequence is: count-in, root note, count-in, melody. There will be a short gap for you to practise after you have heard the test for the second time. You will hear the count-in and root note for the third time followed by a *vocal* count-in and you will then play the melody to the bass and drum backing. The tempo is ♩=90.

Example 1

Please note: The test shown is an example: The assessor will give you a different version in the assessment

Example 2

Please note: The test shown is an example: The assessor will give you a different version in the assessment

Example 3

Please note: The test shown is an example: The assessor will give you a different version in the assessment

Test 2: Harmonic Recall

The assessor will play you a tonic chord followed by a four measure chord sequence in the key of F major played to a bass and drum backing. The sequence will use the I, IIm, IIIm, IV, V and VIm chords. The I and IV chords can be either major or major 7 chords. You will be asked to play the chord sequence to the bass and drum backing in the rhythm show in the example below. This rhythm will be used in all examples of this test given in the assessment. You will then be asked to identify the sequence you have played to the assessor, including any chord extensions. You will hear the test twice.

Each time the test is played the sequence is: count-in, tonic, count-in, chords. There will be a short gap for you to practise after you have heard the test for the second time. You will hear the count-in and tonic for the third time followed by a *vocal* count-in and you will then play the chords to the bass and drum backing. You should then name the chords, including any extensions. The tempo is ♩= 90.

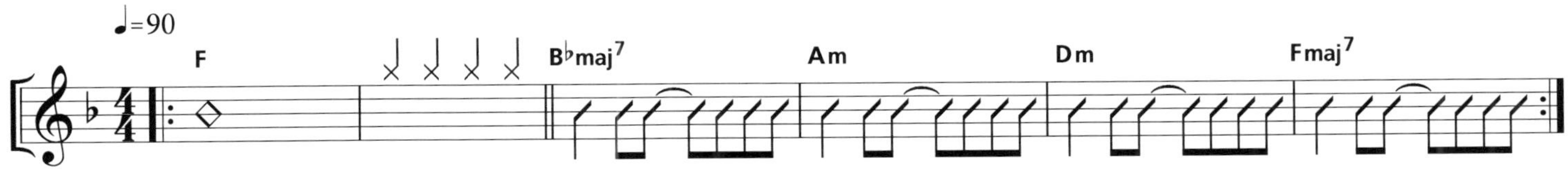

Please note: The test shown is an example: The assessor will give you a different version in the assessment

Section 3 | General Musicianship Questions

In this part of the assessment you will be asked five questions. Four of these questions will be about general music knowledge and the fifth question asked will be about instrumental & technical knowledge.

Music Knowledge
The assessor will ask you four music knowledge questions based on a piece of music that you have played in the assessment. You will nominate the piece of music about which the questions will be asked.

In Level/Grade 8 you will be asked about:

- The names of pitches

- Any expressive musical marking found in the piece such as palm muting, accents, *staccato*, *legato*, *vibrato*, natural and artificial harmonics

- Any dynamic marking found in the piece

- One type of scale that can be used appropriately in the solo section of the piece you have played and its relation to the underlying harmony of the piece (if relevant)
  or:
  How you developed a section of the piece (if relevant)
  or:
  A stylistic feature of the piece characteristic of its genre

Technical Knowledge
The assessor will also ask you one question regarding a technical consideration of your piece, in relation to

- Picking hand: Strumming or picking technique for a short phrase (up to one measure) – demonstration is acceptable
- Fretting hand: Fretting position and fingering used to play a short phrase (up to one measure) – demonstration is acceptable

The assessor will choose the section of music and will ask you to give a brief explanation as to why the technique was appropriate for the chosen section.

About Rockschool Assessments

Entering Rockschool Assessments

Entering a Rockschool assessment is easy, just go online and follow our simple six step process. All details for entering online, dates, fees, regulations and Free Choice Pieces can be found at *www.rslawards.com*

- All candidates should ensure they bring their own Level/Grade syllabus book to the assessment or have proof of digital purchase ready to show the assessor.

Syllabus Guides

You can find further details about Rockschool's Ukulele syllabus by downloading the syllabus guide from our website: *www.rslawards.com*

All candidates should download and read the accompanying syllabus guide when using this level/grade book. Please note that clarifications and updates to syllabus guides are noted at the back of each document.

Performance and Technical Guidance

Students, candidates and teachers may find the following guidance helpful in using the level/grade book and preparing for a Rockschool assessment. Please see below.

- **Tuning**
  Pieces and technical tests have been arranged for re-entrant tuned ukuleles. This is specifically to prepare for the specific techniques which build through the syllabus. If you wish to take a Rockschool assessment using an alternative standard tuning, please contact Rockschool.

- **Fingering**
  Any fingering annotation is given as a guide only. Tablature positions are also given for guidance, except where stipulated to achieve the required technical outcomes (for example, in *campanella* passages).

- **Interpretation**
  Notation should be performed as written, except where there are performance indications to *ad lib. / improvise / develop*, etc. In these instances, the candidate will be marked on their ability to interpret the music in a stylistically appropriate way, commensurate with the level/grade level.

- **Adaptation**
  A small degree of adaptation is allowed where, for example, hand stretches do not facilitate the required notated parts. Marks may be deducted if adaptation results in over-simplification of the notation. If in doubt you can submit any adaptation enquiries to: *info@rslawards.com*
  Further adaptation (for example, alternative solos) will be marked according to the equivalent outcomes achieved.

- **Articulation & Dynamics**
  Where articulation and dynamics are marked on the notation, they should be followed. Where it is open to interpretation, the candidate is free to take their own approach, in accordance with the style of the piece.

- **Chord Symbols**
  Most Hit Tune arrangements have chord symbols written above the notation. This is purely for guidance, and to assist the candidate and teacher. Some pieces (for example, film score arrangements) do not contain chord symbol information, as is more customary with these kinds of scores.

Marking Schemes

Debut to Level/Grade 5 *

ELEMENT	PASS	MERIT	DISTINCTION
Performance Piece 1	12–14 out of 20	15–17 out of 20	18+ out of 20
Performance Piece 2	12–14 out of 20	15–17 out of 20	18+ out of 20
Performance Piece 3	12–14 out of 20	15–17 out of 20	18+ out of 20
Technical Exercises	9–10 out of 15	11–12 out of 15	13+ out of 15
Sight Reading *or* Improvisation & Interpretation	6 out of 10	7–8 out of 10	9+ out of 10
Ear Tests	6 out of 10	7–8 out of 10	9+ out of 10
General Musicianship Questions	3 out of 5	4 out of 5	5 out of 5
TOTAL MARKS	60%+	74%+	90%+

Levels/Grades 6–8

ELEMENT	PASS	MERIT	DISTINCTION
Performance Piece 1	12–14 out of 20	15–17 out of 20	18+ out of 20
Performance Piece 2	12–14 out of 20	15–17 out of 20	18+ out of 20
Performance Piece 3	12–14 out of 20	15–17 out of 20	18+ out of 20
Technical Exercises	9–10 out of 15	11–12 out of 15	13+ out of 15
Quick Study Piece	6 out of 10	7–8 out of 10	9+ out of 10
Ear Tests	6 out of 10	7–8 out of 10	9+ out of 10
General Musicianship Questions	3 out of 5	4 out of 5	5 out of 5
TOTAL MARKS	60%+	74%+	90%+

Performance Certificates | Debut to Level/Grade 8 *

ELEMENT	PASS	MERIT	DISTINCTION
Performance Piece 1	12–14 out of 20	15–17 out of 20	18+ out of 20
Performance Piece 2	12–14 out of 20	15–17 out of 20	18+ out of 20
Performance Piece 3	12–14 out of 20	15–17 out of 20	18+ out of 20
Performance Piece 4	12–14 out of 20	15–17 out of 20	18+ out of 20
Performance Piece 5	12–14 out of 20	15–17 out of 20	18+ out of 20
TOTAL MARKS	60%+	75%+	90%+

* Note that there are no Debut Vocal assessments.

Ukulele Notation Explained

THE MUSICAL STAVE shows pitches and rhythms and is divided by lines into measures. Pitches are named after the first seven letters of the alphabet.

TABLATURE graphically represents the ukulele fingerboard. Each horizontal line represents a string, and each number represents a fret.

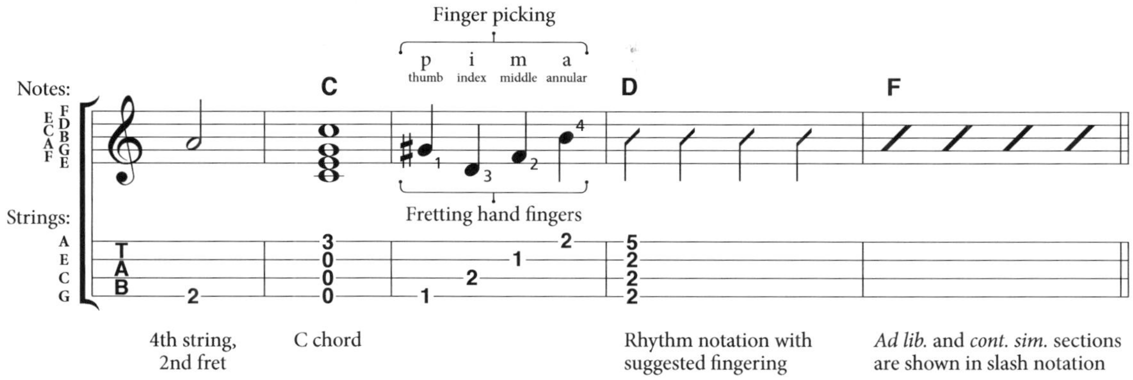

Definitions For Ukulele Notation

HAMMER-ON: Play the lower note, then sound the higher note by fretting it without repicking.

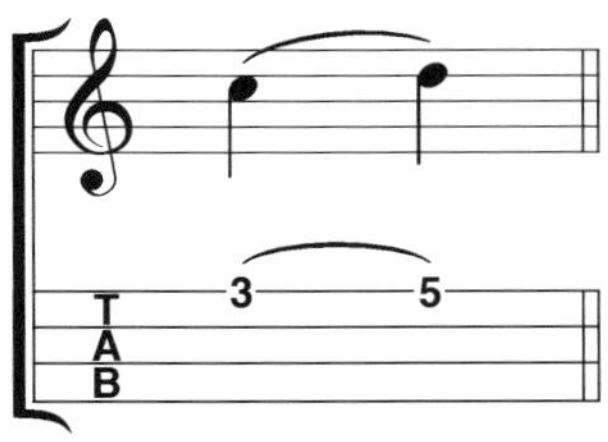

PULL-OFF: Play the higher note then sound the lower note by lifting the finger without repicking.

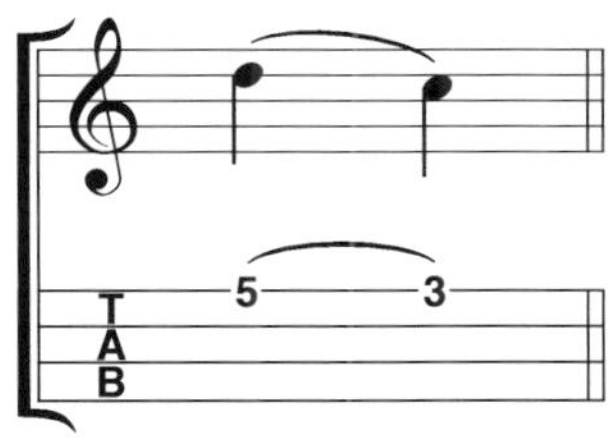

SLIDE: Play the first note, then slide to the next with the same finger.

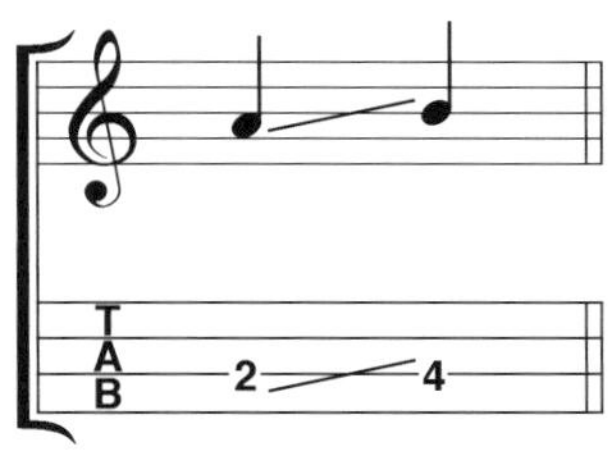

STRING BENDS: Play the first note then bend up or bend down (release the bend) to the pitch indicated in brackets.

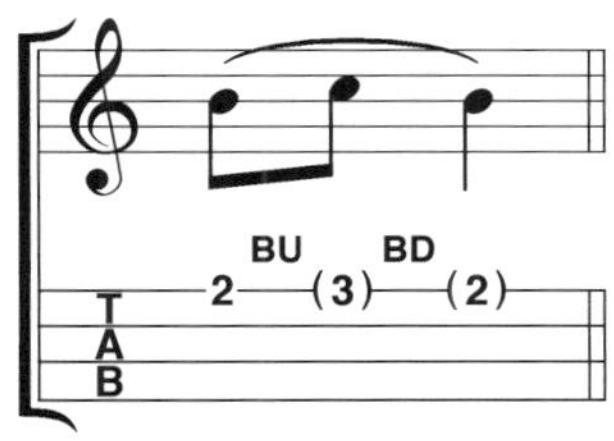

GLISSANDO: A small slide off of a note toward the end of its rhythmic duration. Do not slide 'into' the following note – subsequent notes should be repicked.

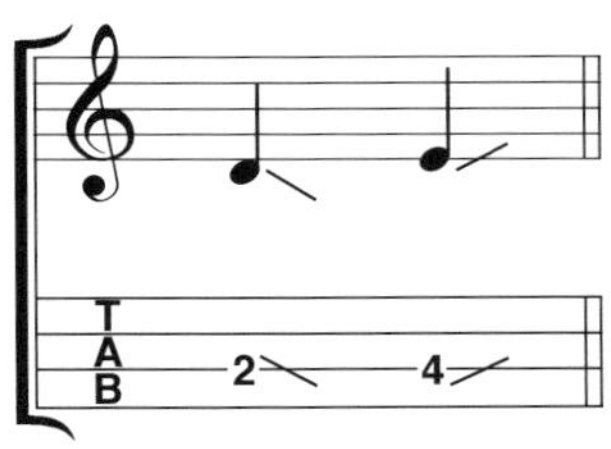

DOWNSTROKE: When using a pick, this symbol indicates a downstroke.

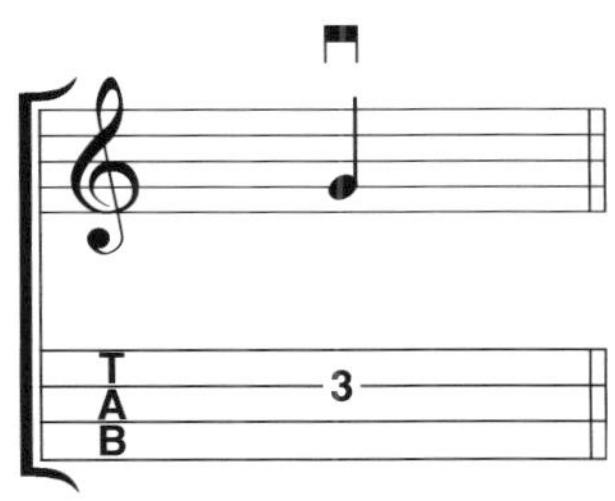

UPSTROKE: When using a pick, this symbol indicates an upstroke.

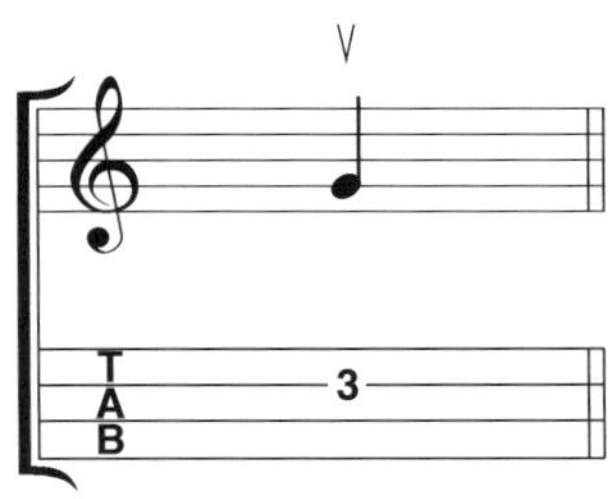

D.𝄋. al Coda

- Go back to the sign (𝄋), then play until the measure marked ***To Coda*** 𝄌 then skip to the section marked 𝄌 ***Coda***.

D.C. al Fine

- Go back to the beginning of the song and play until the measure marked ***Fine*** (end).

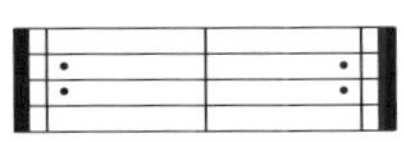

- Repeat the measures between the repeat signs.

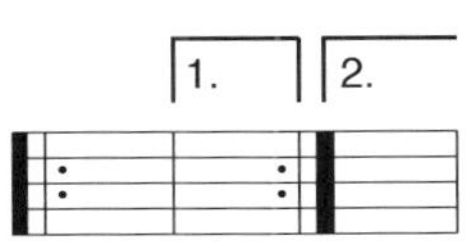

- When a repeated section has different endings, play the first ending only the first time and the second ending only the second time.

Copyright Information

Fire
(Gardner)
Taimane Tauiliili Bobbie Gardner

Bohemian Rhapsody
Words and Music by Freddie Mercury
EMI Music Publishing Ltd.

Cinema Paradiso
(Morricone/Morricone)
EMI General Music SRL

Holier Than Thou
(Hetfield/Ulrich)
Universal Music Publishing Ltd.

Rather Be
(Chatto/Patterson/Marshall/Napier)
Sony / ATV Music Publishing (UK) Ltd. / Songs of Downtown

Spain
(Corea)
Universal / MCA Music Ltd.

mcps